Expository Outlines from Luke

Croft M. Pentz

BAKER BOOK HOUSE
Grand Rapids, Michigan

ISBN 0-8010-6991-2

Printed in the United States of America

FOREWORD

These thirty-nine outlines cover most of the Book of Luke. They are not meant in any way to be a commentary on this book. Rather, they are just a guide for the pastor and teacher to use in teaching this Gospel.

These outlines could be used as a midweek Bible study. They might be used as Sunday school lessons.

In these outlines, we have just touched the high points. Some outlines contain many truths and could be broken down into several messages.

As always, we have kept the outlines very simple. The Bible is a simple book. The outlines are simple enough for the new convert to understand. Yet the mature Christian will be led into new understanding by their use.

It is our prayer that these outlines will be blessed of God to reach the unconverted, as well as help the mature Christian draw near unto God.

–Croft M. Pentz

CONTENTS

1
JOHN THE BAPTIST'S BIRTH PROMISED

Luke 1:5-19

Zacharias was a priest. He was a spiritual man. He was humble and poor. He and his wife had no children. Both now are growing old. He had been faithful to God all his life. God does bless those who are faithful to Him. Faithfulness shows: (1) concern for God, (2) consecration to God.

I. THE PEOPLE—Luke 1:5-7
   1. Characters—v. 5. The priest Zacharias and his wife Elisabeth.
   2. Clean—v. 6. The lives of Zacharias and Elisabeth.
      a) They were righteous.
      b) They walked in all the commandments.
      c) They were blameless—free from reproach.
   3. Childless—v. 7. This presented a problem, since being childless was a reproach to the Jews.

II. THE PURITY—Luke 1:8-12
   1. Work—vv. 8-9. Zacharias is busy about his work in the temple in the burning of incense. They did this twice a day, in the morning and at 3:00 P.M. (Exod. 30:7-8).
   2. Worship—v. 10. All the people were praying at the time of the incense. (Remember this was before the birth of Christ.)
   3. Wonder—vv. 11-12. The angel appears unto Zacharias. Zacharias is fearful. He falls on his face before the Lord. This showed respect to God.

III. THE PROMISE—Luke 1:13-17
   1. Promise—v. 13. Zacharias and Elisabeth are to have a son. His name will be John, meaning "The Lord is gracious or shows grace."
   2. Prophecy—vv. 14-17
      a) Rejoicing—v. 14. Many will rejoice at his birth. His birth will be a blessing to many people.
      b) Righteous—v. 15. He will be great—he will not drink any strong drink.
      c) Repentance—v. 16. Many will turn to God through John the Baptist's preaching.
      d) Revival—v. 17. John will prepare the way for Christ.

IV. THE POWER—Luke 1:18-19

1. Problem—v. 18. Zacharias and Elisabeth are old. Seems impossible to have a son.
2. Power—v. 19. Gabriel the angel, "the mighty one of God," had been sent by God to tell Zacharias this news.

John the Baptist had a very good heritage. Both Zacharias and Elisabeth were godly parents. The life the parents live has an effect on their children. The greatest gifts parents can give their children is to live a godly life daily in their homes.

2
AN ANGEL APPEARS TO MARY

Luke 1:20-38

Since the first promise of the Messiah in Genesis 3:15, the prophets and people had looked forward to the coming Messiah. Many prophecies were given. Now an angel appears unto Mary, telling how she would be the mother of the Son of God, the Messiah.

I. DIVINE PLAN—vv. 20-25
   1. Doubt—v. 20. Zacharias was made dumb because of his doubt. It is necessary to have faith to please God (Heb. 11:6).
   2. Detained—vv. 21-22. Zacharias stayed a long time in the temple. When he came out, he was speechless.
   3. Divine—vv. 23-25. Elisabeth conceives, and now will have a son.

II. DIVINE PROPHECY—vv. 26-33
   1. Place—v. 26. The angel Gabriel, is sent to the city of Galilee.
   2. Person—v. 27. An angel appears to Mary, who was engaged to be married to Joseph.
   3. Personality—v. 28. Mary is highly favored of the Lord, and is blessed among women.
   4. Peace—vv. 29-30
      a) Fear—v. 29. Mary is filled with a godly fear.
      b) Favor—v. 30. She has found favor with God.
   5. Prophecy—vv. 31-33
      a) Son—v. 31. Mary is to have a son—the fulfillment of Genesis 3:15

b) Savior—vv. 32-33. Son of the highest (see Isa. 9:6).

III. DIVINE POWER—vv. 34-38

1. Problem—v. 34. Mary is puzzled. How could she have a son, since she does not know a man? Not a doubtful question, but a request for information.
2. Power—v. 35. The Holy Spirit will come upon Mary, and the child will be of the Holy Ghost. Note: The Son of God!
3. Possibility—vv. 36-37.
   a) Power—v. 36. Elisabeth and Zacharias are to have a son in their old age. Mary also will bear a child.
   b) Possibility—v. 37. With God, all things are possible.
4. Pleasure—v. 38. Mary is willing to accept with pleasure God's will in this matter.

By man's evaluation, Mary was perhaps the most unlikely person to become the mother of the Messiah. This is how God works. What seems unlikely to man is accepted by God. Man does not see as God sees. He looks beyond the outward appearance. He sees the hidden ability and the surrender of the person, and He uses this person.

3
MARY VISITS ELISABETH
Luke 1:39-56

God carefully chose the parents of John the Baptist. Through the proper parents and training, God would use John to lead many people to Christ. Zacharias had prayed that he and Elisabeth would have a son, just as Abraham had prayed that he and Sarah would have a son. With Mary, it was quite different—she was a virgin. Christ's conception would be miraculous. Mary accepts this, and becomes the mother of Jesus.

I. THE PEOPLE—vv. 39-45

1. Reaction—vv. 39-40. After the angel appears to Mary, she goes to her cousin, Elisabeth.
2. Recognition—v. 41. Mary has been accepted of God. Mary was not perfect. She was a human being like all people.

3. Rejoicing—vv. 42-44. Elisabeth rejoices that Mary (the mother of Jesus) would come to visit her.
4. Respect—v. 45. God had respect for Mary, permitting her to become the mother of Jesus.

Mary was a good woman. She was chosen of God. She was not perfect. She, like all people (Rom. 3:23), was born a sinner. To say otherwise would be unscriptural.

II. THE PRAISE—vv. 46-50

1. Rejoicing—vv. 46-47. Mary praises and worships the Lord.
2. Recognition—v. 48
   a) Elisabeth recognizes Mary as the mother of her Lord.
   a) The child to be born is the promised Messiah.
3. Righteousness—vv. 49-50. Mary lifts her voice in praise and worship unto God. Mary never told anyone to worship her. Christ never told anyone to worship Mary. The disciples did not worship Mary, nor tell anyone to worship her.

The Bible teaches that man should worship only the Trinity! We may respect men and women, but we must never worship them.

III. THE PURPOSE—vv. 51-56

1. Power—v. 51. "How powerful is His mighty arm! How He scatters the proud and haughty ones!" (LB).
2. Purpose—v. 52. If man doesn't humble himself—God will humble him. We should always be humble before God.
3. Provision—v. 53. God has always been faithful to meet man's needs.
4. Prophecy—vv. 54-55. God's promise to Abraham.
5. Plan—v. 56. Mary stays with Elisabeth for three months.

Mary is an excellent example of dedication, purity, and humility. She had a love for God's Word. She was obedient to the Lord. Because she loved God, she knew it was God's will that she be the mother of Jesus. This caused her to praise the Lord. Knowing God's Word, and obeying it, produces praise.

4
BIRTH OF JOHN THE BAPTIST
Luke 1:57-76

John the Baptist was one of the greatest men that ever lived. He would be like the Old Testament prophets—Elijah, Isaiah, and Jeremiah (Matt. 14:5). Jesus said there was not a greater prophet born than John the Baptist (Luke 7:28). Zacharias was filled with praise to God for answered prayer. The early years of John the Baptist were guided by Spirit-filled parents.

I. THE SON—Luke 1:57-63
1. Son—v. 57. John the Baptist is born.
2. Shewing—v. 58. All the friends show their kindness to Elisabeth. Do we show kindness? Do we help others? Do we rejoice with those who rejoice and weep with those who weep?
3. Spirit—vv. 59-61. Some people want to call the baby "Zacharias" but Elisabeth insists his name be John.
4. Signs—vv. 62-63. Zacharias cannot speak. They make signs to him. (It is not known if he was deaf or not. We know only that he could not speak.) He asks for a tablet and writes the name "John."

II. THE SPIRITUAL—Luke 1:64-66
1. Praise—v. 64. Zacharias's tongue is loosed, now he speaks and praises God. How much do we praise the Lord? It is so easy to complain and grumble. . . . Let's start praising the Lord more!
2. Promotion—v. 65. This news spreads all over the area. This brings about reverence toward God. How we need to spread Good News! Too often we are quick to believe and spread bad news.
3. Purity—v. 66. People begin to ask, "What manner of child shall this be?" When God blesses, it causes people to ask questions! God's hand would be upon John in a special way!

III. THE SPEAKING—Luke 1:67-76
1. Prophecy—v. 67. The Holy Spirit comes upon Zacharias and he prophecies.
2. Praise—v. 68. "Praise the Lord, the God of Israel, for He has come to visit His people and has redeemed them" (LB).
3. Person—vv. 69-70."He is sending us a Mighty Savior from the royal line of His servant David, just as He promised through His holy prophets long ago" (LB).

4. Protection—v. 71. He would save us and protect us from our enemies—our one main enemy—Satan.
5. Promise—vv. 72-73. "He has been merciful to our ancestors, yes, to Abraham himself, by remembering His sacred promise to him" (LB).
6. Privilege—v. 74. We have the privilege of serving God.
7. Purity—Only Christ can make us holy and pure.
8. Prophet—v. 76. John, a prophet will prepare the way for Christ.

John the Baptist had a great ministry ahead of him. He would prepare the way for Christ, the promised Messiah. We too may help prepare the way for the Lord. Our lives can be a blessing in preparing people to accept Christ as Savior. John introduced Christ to the people. We too can introduce men and women to Christ.

5
THE CHRISTMAS MESSAGE
Luke 2:1-20

The Christmas story never grows old. It is fresh every year. It is not a holiday—it's a holy day. Without Christ, there would be no Christmas. Christmas is the birthday of Jesus. It's easy to be so busy we crowd Christ out of our Christmas.

I. THE SON—vv. 1-7
   1. Situation—vv. 1-7. Mary and Joseph go to pay their taxes.
   2. Son of God (see John 3:16). God gave us His best.
   3. Son of Man (Phil. 2:6-11). See His character in Isaiah 9:6. Note five of His characteristics.

II. THE SHEPHERDS—vv. 8-10
   1. The working—v. 8. They are busy keeping their sheep.
   2. The wonder—v. 9. The glory of God comes down to these humble shepherds. They are fearful.
   3. The word—v. 10
      a) News—"Fear not: for behold I bring you good tidings of great joy.
      b) Nature—"Which shall be to all people."

III. THE SAVIOR—v. 11.

1. Place—City of David, meaning the city of Bethlehem.
2. Person—A Savior. The promised Messiah of the Old Testament is now born—the One the prophets had told of and to whose coming they had looked forward.

IV. THE SIGN—v. 12

Jesus is born in a stable among the animals.

1. Jesus was born in a humble place—in a manger, among the cows and donkeys.
2. Jesus lived humbly—He had no permanent home.
3. Jesus died a humble death—upon a cross.
4. Jesus was buried in a humble way—in a borrowed tomb.

V. THE SONG—vv. 13-14

1. The praising—v. 13. The angels sing praise to God. Do we give praise to God? The best way to thank God is to praise Him.
2. The peace—v. 14. Peace on earth to all men. The promised Prince of Peace in Isaiah 9:6 now has come. Praising God will bring us peace. The world cannot have peace until they have Christ.

VI. THE SEEKING—vv. 15-17

1. The plan—v. 15. The shepherds want to go and see the Christ. Do you have a desire to be with Him?
2. The people—v. 16. They come and see Joseph and Mary and Jesus. We see Christ through faith, prayer, and the Bible.
3. The preaching—v. 17. They go out and tell others about Christ.

VII.THE SPREADING—vv. 18-20

1. The wonder—v. 18. People hear of the miracle and wonder.
2. The worship—v. 19. Mary worshiped the Lord.
3. The witness—v. 20. Shepherds praise God and tell others.

Christ has come! His birth, life, death, resurrection, and ascension bring joy to us all. If we want joy, we must have Christ. He came to give joy and peace to all people. If we have Christ, then we have joy. Without Christ we cannot have joy, peace, or satisfaction. Do you have Christ?

6

THE CALL TO THE DISCIPLES

Luke 5:1-11

There were many people who followed Christ. They followed Him for many different reasons. Some brought their friends to see Him. During the first year of His ministry, some followed Him from time to time. They were part-time disciples. They went back to their fish nets. At first Christ called Peter, Andrew, James, and John. The second time Christ calls these four, they leave their nets and become full-time disciples.

I. THE PLACE—vv. 1-2.

1. Attitude—v. 1. Many follow Christ. He stands by a lake to speak. Lake Gennesaret is also known as the Sea of Galilee.
2. Ambition—v. 2. The fishermen were busy washing their nets. God cannot work through lazy people.
   - a) Laziness is sin! We should not be lazy (Rom. 12:11).
   - b) Indifference is sin! God does not approve of this (Matt. 25:26-30).
   - c) "Don't care" attitude is sin (compare James 4:17).

Don't be lazy at your job. Don't be lazy about reading your Bible and praying. Laziness keeps you from having God's best. It keeps you from growing in Christ. It hinders the church from growing.

II. THE PERSON—vv. 3-9

1. Preaching—v. 3. He teaches, or preaches, from a boat. The people gather on the shore to listen.
2. People—v. 4. Christ tells Simon to go out into the deep water and let down the net for a draught.
3. Problem—v. 5. Peter had fished all night and had caught nothing. There seemed to be no hope, but he is willing to obey Christ's command. *Do we fully obey Christ in all things?*
4. Prospects—v. 6. There are so many fish that the nets begin to break. This came because of obedience.
5. Partners—v. 6. They call their partners to help them. Both ships are filled. *Obey what Christ says!*
6. Personal—vv. 8-9. Peter confesses his wrong. He did not really believe Christ. Now he is ashamed.

III. THE PEOPLE—vv. 10-11

1. Desire—v. 10. Christ tells Peter not to be fearful. Now he would catch men, meaning he would be a soul winner. Up to this time he had caught fish, now he would lead men to Christ.

2. Determination—v. 11.
   a) Forsaking—"They forsook all"—leaving family and friends.
   b) Following—They follow Christ (compare Luke 9:23).

Christ today calls people. However, many are "spiritually deaf" and they do not hear the voice of Christ. Following Christ involves four important things—

1. Desire. We have a choice. No one forces us to follow Christ.
2. Denial. We must forget our selfish plans and desires.
3. Dedication. Christ must have all of us . . . fully dedicated to Him.
4. Determination. Determined daily to serve and follow Him all the way.

Christ is calling. . . . Will you follow Him? If not, you'll follow sin, self, and Satan!

7
FORGIVENESS AND HEALING
Luke 5:12-26

Christ came to give life. He's interested not only in the soul of man, but the body as well. The body is the temple of the Holy Spirit (I Cor. 6:19). Only God can save the soul (John 14:6). Only God can heal the body. Though we have good physicians and medication, it still is God who does the healing.

I. THE FAITH—vv. 12-16
   1. Complaint—v. 12. This man has leprosy. He knew Jesus' ability to heal, but questions His willingness.
   2. Concern—v. 13. Jesus says, "I will," and the man is healed immediately. Surely this man had faith in Christ.
   3. Charged—v. 14. Go show yourself to the priest, so he can confirm the healing to all people.
   4. Congregation—v. 15. A great multitude come to hear Him, as well as to be healed.
   5. Communion—v. 16. Jesus leaves the crowd for a time of secret prayer (note Matt. 6:6).

II. THE FAVOR—vv. 17-20

1. Popularity—v. 17. People come from all over the area to be healed. Note that the power of the Lord was present to heal, God meets the hungry heart.
2. Person—v. 18. A sick man is brought to Jesus by his friends.
3. Persistence—v. 19. They cannot reach Jesus because of the large crowd. These men do not give up. They make a hole in the roof and let the man down in front of Jesus.
4. Pardon—v. 20. Jesus forgives the man's sin. He forgives man from all sin (I John 1:7).

All Christians need the same persistence that the men who brought the sick man to Jesus had. Never give up. Keep trying.

III. THE FORGIVENESS—vv. 21-26

1. Complaint—v. 21. The Pharisees ask, Who can forgive sin, except God? They do not accept Christ being equal with God.
2. Comparison—vv. 22-23. Jesus knows their hearts. He asks, "Which is easier? to say, Thy sins be forgiven thee, or take up thy bed and walk?"
3. Christ—v. 24. The Son of man (also Son of God) has power to forgive sin (I John 1:7, Rom. 10:13). The man is commanded to rise and walk.
4. Complete—vv. 25-26.
   a) Restored—v. 25. Man is made whole spiritually and physically.

   b) Rejoicing—v. 26. People praise the Lord and respect God.

As the Pharisees opposed Christ's power to forgive and heal, so today some religious leaders oppose God's saving and healing power. Though many see God at work, they still reject His power. Despite this, many accept Him, and enjoy God's changing power.

8

CHRIST CHANGES MAN'S LIFE

Luke 5:27-39

Note three things in this lesson: (1) Christ calls man to do His work. God is dependent upon man to accomplish His work. (2) He takes time to eat with sinners. He is interested in their souls. (3) He explains the importance of new life in Christ, opposing the self-righteous Pharisees, who depended on their own good works.

I. THE CALL—vv. 27-29

1. Call—v. 27. Jesus calls Levi (Matthew), a publican. These people were not respected (Matt. 5:46; Mark 2:15-16).
2. Consecration—v. 28. Matthew leaves all and follows. He gives up a good income. He asks no questions, makes no demands—he simply follows Christ!
3. Company—v. 29. Matthew gives a large feast for Jesus and many attend. Zacchaeus did the same thing (Luke 19:5-7). This was perhaps a means of telling others what had happened to him, as well as an effort to win souls.

God still calls man today, He still seeks for man (Ezek. 22:30). Many ignore the call.

II. THE COMPLAINT—vv. 30-32

1. Sinners—v. 30. The Pharisees criticize Jesus for eating with sinners. As Christians, we should hate sin, but love the sinner. Christians should not isolate themselves completely from the sinner. They should not take part in their deeds, but they should love them.
2. Sick—v. 31. Those who are sick with sin need help—not those who are well. This is why Christ spent time with the sinner. Often time is spent with Christians that should be used to reach the sinner and win him to Christ.
3. Salvation—v. 32. Christ came to save sinners. The ministry of Christians should be directed to the sinner (note the words of Jesus [Mark 16:15; John 15:16]).

III. THE COMPARISON—vv. 33-39

1. Complain—vv. 33-35. Complaint of feasting and not fasting. No one fasts during times of joy. We fast during times of sorrow and need and trouble.
2. Comparison—vv. 36-37. A parable, comparing the old religion

(man's way) with the new religion (Christ's way). Note the two comparisons:

a) Putting patches on old garments. Salvation is putting on Christ—not patches. He makes us new (II Cor. 5:17).

b) Putting new wine in old bottles. Wine is a picture of gladness. Only Christ can give joy (Ps. 16:11).

3. Conversion—vv. 38-39. Salvation changes the life. There is no patch up—it's made new. No one wants to go back to his old way after tasting salvation.

Christ can, and does, change men's lives. The new birth (John 3:1-8) changes man completely. He is made new through salvation (II Cor. 5:17). Christ changes the: (1) attitudes, (2) affections, (3) actions, (4) ambitions. Let Him change you.

9
THE POWERFUL CHRIST
Luke 6:1-19

Christ is all powerful. In this lesson we see His power over: (1) Pharisees and critics; (1) sickness, by healing the withered hand; and (3) evil spirits, or demons. This power came from God as He spent time alone with God in prayer.

I. THE POWER—vv. 1-5

1. Sabbath—v. 1. Jesus and the disciples go through the corn fields (really wheat) on the sabbath.
2. Skeptics—v. 2. The Pharisees complain about Jesus and the disciples harvesting on the sabbath, since the Jewish laws prohibited this.
3. Scriptures—vv. 3-4. Jesus used Old Testament Scriptures to show how David ate the shewbread, reserved for the priests only. This simply means: Life is more important than the rules of man.
4. Savior—v. 5. Jesus is the sabbath, or above the sabbath.

II. THE PERFECTION—vv. 6-11

1. Person—v. 6. Jesus enters the synagogue on the sabbath, and teaches. There is a man with a withered hand.

2. Plan—v. 7. Pharisees watch to see if Christ will heal on the sabbath so they can accuse Him.
3. Power—vv. 8-10. Christ knows their thoughts. Jesus asks the man to stand. He then asks if it lawful to do good or evil on the sabbath. Jesus tells the man, "Stretch forth thy hand."
4. Plot—v. 11. Because Jesus heals the man, the Pharisees seek a way to destroy Christ.

III. THE PREPARATION—vv. 12-16
Christ calls the disciples, and begins to prepare them to carry forth His work.
1. Prayer—v. 12. Jesus prays all night before He chooses the disciples. His private prayers were long, but His public prayers were short.
2. People—v. 13. He chose twelve men to carry on His work. He knew their abilities and limitations, and chose accordingly.

IV. THE POPULARITY—vv. 17-19
1. People—v. 17. The people come from many areas to be healed by Christ. The disciples are with Him, learning from Him.
2. Power—v. 18. People with unclean spirits come and are healed. People oppressed by Satan are freed. People who are depressed by Satan are freed. People who are possessed by Satan are freed!
3. Pity—v. 19. People seek to touch Him. He heals all. He shows concern.

Christ calls the disciples to do His work. Note the power He gives them to do this work (Mark 16:15-18). They obey Him, with astounding results (Mark 16:20). Later, in the Book of Acts, we see His followers changing the world.

10
OBEYING GOD'S WORD
Luke 6:20-49

To be a success in the Christian life, a person must have a good foundation. When the storms of life come, you must depend upon God's Word. Many Bible scholars believe this portion of the Scripture is equal to Matthew 5—7, known as The Sermon on the Mount. Perhaps we could say there are three types of Christians: (1) successful Christians with a good foundation, (2) carnal Christians with a shaky foundation, and (3) backsliding Christian with no foundatin.

I. DIVINE ATTITUDES—Luke 6:20-26
   1. The poor—v. 20. Hungry for spiritual things.
   2. The promise—v. 21. Satisfied, or being filled with joy.
   3. The persecution—v. 22. Compare this with II Timothy 3:12 and Matthew 5:10-12. Also see Romans 8:18.
   4. The prophets—v. 23. The prophets suffered much. See Hebrews 11:33-40.
   5. The plight—vv. 24-25. Sorrow for the rich—they have material gain but no spiritual gain.
   6. The problem—v. 26. You cannot please all people. When you live right, your life will disturb other people.

II. DIVINE AFFECTION—vv. 27-36
   1. Patient with enemies—v. 27. Note two things: love your enemies and be good to them.
   2. Pray for your enemies—v. 28. Praise them. This will require divine love (I Cor. 13:4-7).
   3. Peace with enemies—vv. 29-36. Accept persecution. Give up things, if it will bring peace. Treat others as you want to be treated. Give of yourself and possessions. Live differently from the non-Christian.

III. DIVINE EFFECT—vv. 37-45
   1. Practice—vv. 37-38. Don't judge others. Be forgiving. Give, and God will give to you.
   2. Parable—v. 39. Can an undedicated person lead a sinner to Christ? Of course not. You must be dedicated to the Lord to be effective.
   3. Perfection—v. 40. Choose Christ as your Master. Don't listen to false teachers.
   4. Patience—vv. 41-42. It is wrong to judge others (see Matt. 7:1-5).
   5. Practical—vv. 43-45. A Christian is known by his actions. Out of the heart the mouth speaks.

IV. DIVINE ATTENTION—Luke 6:46-49
   1. Fakery—v. 46. If we call Him "Lord," then we must obey Him. The word "Lord" means that He is our boss—He controls us!

2. Faithfulness—v. 47. Those who hear Him and follow Him are like the man who built his house upon the rock—*Nothing coud destroy it!*
3. Failure—v. 48-49. Hearing and not doing is like a man who built his house with no good foundation. Storms easily destroy it.

Have a good foundation—build upon God's Word. Read and practice the Sermon on the Mount (Matt. 5—7). Believe it. Let it become a part of your life. A Christian will follow the Ten Commandments (Exod. 20:1-17; compare with Matt. 5—7). If we cannot follow these simple rules, then we will not make it to heaven!

11

CHRIST DEMONSTRATES HIS POWER

Luke 7:1-17

Christ never preached a funeral sermon. When meeting the dead, He gave them life. He came to give life (John 10:10; 11:25-26). He who has Christ, has life. Without Christ, man is dead in his sins (Eph. 2:1). He gives enjoyable life, but also eternal life.

I. THE HEALING—vv. 1-10
1. Problem—vv. 1-2. Centurion's servant sick and near death.
2. Plea—vv. 3-7. The centurion said he was not worthy to have Christ come to his home: "Just say the word," and the healing will come.
3. Power—v. 8. See the centurion's power.
4. Perfection—vv. 9-10. Jesus sees his faith and heals.

II. THE HORROR—vv. 11-12
1. Place—v. 11. Nain, twenty-one miles north of Capernaum and sixty miles north of Jerusalem.
2. Problem—v. 12. The only son the mother had is now dead. He was being prepared for burial. All hope was gone.

III. THE HOPE—v. 13.
1. The Person—"And when the Lord saw her." Christ sees us. He knows all about us. The things we do, our thoughts and actions.
2. The pity—"He had compassion on her." Jesus always has com-

passion on people (Matt. 9:36). *Do we have compassion for others?*

3. The peace—"Weep not." Christ always brings peace (John 14:27; see also Isa. 26:3; Phil. 4:7).

IV. THE HEALTH—vv. 14-15

1. Concern—"And he came and touched the bier [coffin]." He knew the mother had a broken heart. He cares for us.
2. Constrainment—"And they that bare him stood still." They were interested in what Christ would do. They had seen Him do miracles before.
3. Command—"And he said, young man, I say unto thee, arise." Here we see Christ the Master over death.
4. Complete—v. 15. The dead man comes to life. Christ always brings life. *Only through Christ may we have life!*

V. THE HAPPINESS—vv. 16-17

1. Power—"And there came fear on all." These people were not scared. "Fear" means "respect," or "honor toward God."
2. Praise—"And they glorified God." There is praise when God works and moves in the hearts and lives of people. Salvation which brings new life causes us to praise the Lord.
3. Prophet—"That a great prophet is risen up among you," These were the words of Isaiah 9:6-7 and Deuteronomy 18. Now the people see the "Messiah" in action.
4. People—"That God visited his people." God in the person of Christ.
5. Promotion—vv. 17-18. The good news of the Lord was spread.

Christ wants to give you life. Life while you live, and life after death. After death there is heaven or hell. We have a choice as to where we will go after death. The enjoyable life which Christ gives us on earth leads us to everlasting life. Rejection of this life will mean punishment in hell forever (Mark 16:16).

12
THE COMING MESSIAH
Luke 7:18-35

The promised Messiah comes as it was prophesied. If the Pharisees had believed the Old Testament Scriptures, they would have recognized Jesus as the Messiah. Perhaps deep in their hearts they knew Him to be the Messiah but were unwilling to accept Him.

I. SEEKING—vv. 18-20
  1. Supernatural—v. 18. The disciples of John heard of the supernatural power of Christ.
  2. Savior—vv. 19-20. Was Jesus the Messiah? Or, should they continue to look for the Messiah promised in Genesis 3:15?

II. SAVIOR—vv. 21-23
  1. Supernatural—v. 21. Note the various sicknesses. (1) Infirmities (chronic illnesses). (2) Plagues (communicable diseases). (3) Evil spirits (demon possession). (4) Blindness.
  2. Sharing—v. 22. Go and share with others what you have seen. Share it with others. Spread this good news.
  3. Stability—v. 23. "And tell him, 'Blessed is the one who does not lose his faith in me' " (LB).

III. SUPERNATURAL—vv. 24-29
  1. Personality—vv. 24-25. After they left, Jesus talked to the crowd about John. " 'Who is this man you went out into the Judean wilderness to see?' he asked. 'Did you find him weak as grass, moved by every breath of wind? Did you find him dressed in expensive clothes? No! Men who live in luxury are found in palaces, not out in the wilderness' " (LB).
  2. Prophet—v. 26. Christ is a prophet but more than a prophet.
  3. Prophecy—v. 27. Compare with Isaiah 40:3; Malachi 3:1.
  4. Popularity—v. 28. John was the greatest of prophets because he introduced Jesus; yet all men are the same in God's sight.
  5. Pardon—v. 29. People who hear Christ and accept Him are cleansed from their sin.

IV. STUBBORN—vv. 30-35
  1. Rejection—v. 30. People accept John's preaching and are baptized, except the Pharisees. They reject God's plan for their lives (compare John 1:11).

2. Reaction—vv. 31-34. The Pharisees were not satisfied with John's or Jesus' preaching. They falsely accuse them both.
3. Reply—v. 35. The Pharisees and critics always justify their double standards.

The Messiah has come. Have you accepted Him? We must accept Him not only as Savior, but as Lord and Master as well. We must believe with both the head and the heart (see Rom. 10:9-10). When we receive Him, we become sons of God (John 1:12). He is our Father, and we are brothers and sisters in the Lord.

13

JESUS IS ANOINTED

Luke 7:36-50

Christ is interested in physical death. He is also interested in spiritual death. When the Bible speaks of "spiritual death" it means separation from God. Sin always brings spiritual death. The forgiveness of sins is the greatest of all miracles. In this lesson Christ forgives a woman, and she shows her thanks and praise.

I. THE CRITICISM—vv. 36-39
1. Savior—v. 36. Jesus is invited to eat with the Pharisees. They were a religious group of Jews. Notice that Jesus ate with sinners. We must mix with sinners if we expect to win them to Christ.
2. Sinner—v. 37. A woman who was a prostitute, the worst of sinners, came to see Jesus. She brought an alabaster box of very expensive perfume.
3. Sincere—v. 38. She gave all she had. She washed the feet of Jesus with her tears. She wiped His feet with her hair. She kissed His feet. She anointed His feet with the perfume.
4. Shame—v. 39. The Pharisees were critical of Christ and the woman. Christ loves everyone. He died for all. We should hate sin, but love the sinner.

II. THE CHRIST—vv. 40-47
1. Savior—v. 40. Christ speaks to Simon. (There are many different Simons in the New Testament.)

2. Story—vv. 41-43. Christ uses a story to explain a truth. Christ forgave this woman from many sins, so she was most thankful.
3. Service—vv. 44-46. This woman gave "her all" to Christ.
   a) She gave her savings—all her life savings in perfume.
   b) She gave her service—a good test of Christianity.
   c) She gave herself—she gave herself by worshiping Christ.
4. Sins—v. 47. The woman's sin, which was great, was forgiven by the Lord.

III. THE CONVERSION—vv. 48-50
1. Pardon—v. 48. Christ forgives all sins. His blood forgives and cleanses each sin (I John 1:7; see also Ps. 103:3).
2. Problem—v. 49. The Jews criticized Christ for His claim to forgive sins. They did not accept Christ as the Messiah. Some were blind to the truth—others did not want to accept Christ.
3. Peace—v. 50. Christ forgives the woman's sin. With this pardon comes peace.

Christ can cleanse the worst of sinners. There are none "so bad" that Christ cannot forgive! He can save the "bad sinner" just as easily as He can save the "good sinner." Love for God will cause us to a love the sinner. A person who does not love the sinner does not really love God. A person cannot really get near to Christ without loving the sinner.

14
THE POWER OF THE SOWER

Luke 8:1-25

Jesus often spoke in parables. His teaching was always simple, short, and to the point. Though it was simple, yet it was profound. His teachings have stood the test of time. They have continued down through the years, changing the lives of men, as well as changing communities and nations.

I. PEOPLE—vv. 1-3
1. Preaching—v. 1. Jesus goes through the area, preaching the kingdom of God. The twelve disciples are with Him.
2. People—vv. 2-3. He healed and cast demons out of many who

were possessed, one of these being Mary Magdalene. Joanna and Susanna gave of their substance toward the work of the Lord.

II. PARABLE—vv. 4-8

1. Symbol—v. 4. Jesus speaks through symbols or parables.
2. Sower—vv. 5-8. A sower went forth to sow. Note the types of soil:
   a) Wayside—v. 5. Trodden down, fowls came and ate it.
   b) Rock—v. 6. Sprouted quickly and quickly died.
   c) Among thorns—v. 7. Thorns choke out the new growth.
   d) Good ground—v. 8. Sprang up quickly, one-hundred-fold increase.

III. PICTURE—vv. 9-15

1. Symbol—v. 9. A symbol, or a parable, makes a truth easy for all to understand.
2. Simplicity—v. 10. Christ wanted everyone to understand this parable.
3. Seed—v. 11. The seed is God's Word.
   a) Wayside—v. 12. People hear, but Satan steals the Word away.
   b) Rock—v. 13. Hear but because it has no root the new growth quickly dies.
   c) Thorns—v. 14. The new growth is choked by cares, riches, and pleasures.

IV. PERSONAL—vv. 16-18

1. Reveal—v. 16. When lighting a candle, put it where all can see.
2. Revelation—v. 17. All things done in secret will come to light some day.
3. Responsibilities—v. 18. If we do not use our abilities and talents, they will be taken from us.

V. POWER—vv. 19-25

1. Comparison—vv. 19-21. All who hear and obey His Word are members of God's family.
2. Concern—vv. 22-23. Storm arises. Jesus is asleep on a boat; the disciples are filled with fear.
3. Control—vv. 24-25. Jesus is wakened. He rebukes the water. Note: "Where is your faith?" He controls the wind and waves.

Christ wants all Christians to be like the good soil—producing good results. If all Christians were like this, we would leave such an impact on the world that the world would soon be changed. Don't allow Satan to steal away *your* seed.

15
THE TRANSFIGURATION
Luke 9:28-56

As Peter, James, and John were with Jesus, they saw Him transfigured. One who prays will see his own life changed by the power of God. Also, He will prepare us for the tasks we must fulfill. Without prayer, we are useless and helpless.

I. CHANGE—vv. 28-36
1. Seeking—v. 28. Jesus takes Peter, James, and John to the mountain to pray.
2. Supernatural—vv. 29-31. As He prays, He is transfigured. Moses and Elijah appear: Moses—law; Elijah—prophets.
3. Sleeping—v. 32. The disciples, asleep, now awaken!
4. Selfishness—v. 33. Peter wants to stay there. God gives us His blessings to share with others!
5. Satisfaction—vv. 34-35. God is pleased with His Son.
6. Secret—v. 36. This is all to be kept a secret.

II. CONTROL—vv. 37-43
1. People—v. 37. Many people meet them as they come down.
2. Problem—vv. 38-39. A man possessed with a demon needs help, deliverance.
3. Powerless—v. 40. The disciples had been unable to cast out the demon. They were helpless and powerless.
4. Power—vv. 41-43. Jesus casts out the demon. It took special power to do this.

III. CHILDLIKE—vv. 44-50
1. Prophecy—vv. 44-45. Christ speaks of His death. The disciples do not seem to understand.
2. Pride—vv. 46-48. Selfish pride is shown. Jesus takes a child as an example of true greatness.
3. Personality—vv. 49-50. At times people may not agree on minor points, but if it means advancing the kingdom of God, cooperate and don't oppose.

IV. CONVERSION—vv. 51-56
1. Preparation—vv. 51-52. Messengers go ahead into Samaria to prepare people for Christ's coming.
2. Problem—v. 53. The people do not accept Him.

3. Patience—v. 54. James and John are ready to call fire from heaven to destroy them. They have no patience.
4. Pardon—vv. 55-56. Christ rebukes them. He hadn't come to destroy lives—He came to save lives.

Christ had an answer in every situation. He had the right parable, or example, to teach man in the proper ways. Yet, many refused to accept Him as the Messiah. We might say that they didn't want to accept Him as the Messiah because it would demand a change in their mode of living. living.

16
MISSION OF THE SEVENTY

Luke 9:57-62; 10:1-24

The incidents in this lesson occurred about six months before Jesus went to the cross. He knew His time was short, so He wanted to send out as many workers as possible to reach the lost with the gospel. At first Christ called twelve disciples. They would be the leaders of the church. Then He called the seventy. These seventy workers went out two by two into the towns and villages. Christ still calls today for those who will do His work. *Note the threefold call.*

(1) Call from heaven (Mark 16:15). Witness to all people.
(2) Call from hell (Luke 16:19-31). Warn people about hell.
(3) Call from the heathen (Ps. 142:4). Care for people.

I. WEAK EXCUSES—Luke 9:57-62
1. Divine—vv. 57-58
a) Surrender—v. 57. Is willing to follow the Lord anywhere.
b) Savior—v. 58. Christ has no place as His own home.
2. Delay—vv. 59-60. This man was postponing, making an excuse. When Christ calls—follow! Put Christ first (Matt. 6:33; notice also the words of Jesus in Matt. 10:37).
3. Distraction—vv. 61-62. This man wanted to serve Christ—but not fully! We must be willing to "go all the way" (note v. 62—looking back; compare Phil. 3:13-15).

Do you make excuses when it comes to following the Lord?

II. WISE ENCOURAGEMENT—Luke 10:1-16

1. Pray—vv. 1-2. Before going, we must pray! Many think they can go without praying. This leads to failure and defeat.
2. Go—vv. 3-6. Notice the importance of depending on Christ.
   a) Be meek—Sent as lambs among wolves.
   b) Be dependent—Don't think of money. Think of what you can do.
   c) Be diligent—"Salute no man"—don't talk—get to work!
   d) Be ready—To give peace to those present.
3. Stay—vv. 7-9. If welcomed in the house, then speak. Don't go from house to house—gossiping. Eat what is set before you. Heal the sick—preach the gospel.
4. Leave—vv. 10-16. If not welcomed, don't force yourself upon them. Those who reject will be punished by the Lord.

III. WONDERFUL ENDUEMENT—Luke 10:17-24

1. Divine power—vv. 17-19.
   a) Power over the person of Satan—sly and tricky.
   b) Power over the plan of Satan—His plan is to destroy us!
   c) Power over the power of Satan—His power is greater than ours. (Notice these verses: Rom. 8:31; I John 4:4.)
2. Divine Pleasure—vv. 20-24.
   a) Salvation—v. 20. Rejoice because your names are written in the book.
   b) Spirit—v. 21-24. God reveals His plan to us through His Spirit.

God has called all Christians to do His work (John 15:16). All are called, but few answer this call. Following Christ means that we live like He lived. Talk like He talked. Pray like He prayed. Are you willing to *follow the Lord all the way?*

17

THE GOOD SAMARITAN

Luke 10:25-42

As Christians, we should be willing to help others. Often Christians are so busy with selfish plans that they have no time to help others. In the Christian life, we not only get but we must be willing to give! If you want a real blessing from God—help others.

I. THE SINCERITY—Luke 10:25-29
   1. The desire—v. 25. A man comes to Christ, seeking the way to heaven. Many people are seeking for the truth!
   2. The demand—vv. 26-27.
      a) Love God with all thy heart—feelings!
      b) Love God with all thy soul—spiritual being!
      c) Love God with all thy strength—physical love!
      d) Love God with all thy mind—thought life.
   3. The destiny—v. 28. By keeping this command we are keeping the First Commandment (Exod. 20:1-3). This leads to eternal life.

II. THE STORY—Luke 10:30-35
   1. The problem—v. 30. A traveler was robbed, wounded, and left along the roadside to die.
   2. The people—vv. 31-35. Notice the people who came by:
      a) A PRIEST. He represents the *religious world*. He passed by without helping. Some religious groups are nothing more than clubs.
      b) A LEVITE. He represents the *church world*. The Levite passed by and did not help. Some churches are so busy socially that they have no time to help people spiritually.
      c) A SAMARITAN. He represents the *Christian world*. The Christian who knows Christ personally will be happy to help others.
   3. The pity—Here we see the pity shown by the Samaritan to the wounded traveler, who was left by others to die without help.
      a) Divine love—He had compassion upon him.
      b) Practical love—He bound up his wounds.
      c) Kind love—He took him to an inn to be sheltered and cared for.
      d) Unselfish love—He paid for his care while he recovered.

III. THE SIMPLICITY—Luke 10:36-37

1. Application—v. 36. Who was the neighbor? The one who was wounded. The whole world is our neighbor. They need help. Let's help them!
2. Answer—v. 37. Note Jesus' words: "Go and do thou likewise." Show kindness and love to others. "But if someone who is supposed to be a Christian has money enough to live well, and sees a brother in need, and won't help him—how can God's love be within him?" (I John 3:17, LB).
3. Affection—vv. 38-42. Here we see the importance of love in action. This is what God seeks.

Are you a good Samaritan? Do you help those in need? Do you give *yourself* and *money* to help men find God? Words are empty and cheap if we say we love God, but don't help others. How do you help others? Follow these steps:

1. Be considerate. Think of others—their needs and problems.
2. Be consecrated. When you give yourself to God, you will be helpful.
3. Be compassionate. Put yourself in the place of others.
4. Be Christlike. He loved and helped all people.

18
THE CHRISTIAN AND PRAYER

Luke 11:1-13

Enoch walked with God. Abraham was a man of prayer. Elijah prayed and the fire fell. He prayed again and God sent rain. Moses prayed for forty days, and God gave him the Ten Commandments. Jesus spent whole nights in prayer. He prayed, "Not my will, but thine be done." The Bible tells us to pray at all times (I Thess. 5:17). As the air is to the body, so prayer is to the soul. God answers prayer in three ways: (1) Yes, (2) No, (3) Wait.

I. THE PATTERN OF PRAYER—vv. 1-4

1. Request—v. 1. The disciples ask Jesus to teach them how to pray. You learn *how* to pray by *praying*.
2. Rule of praying—vv. 2-4

a) The Father—"Our Father which art in heaven."
b) The name—"Hallowed [holy] be Thy name."
c) The will—"Thy kingdom come, Thy will be done."
d) The provision—"Give us this day our daily bread." This means daily food, strength, and other provisions.
e) The forgiveness—"Forgive us our sins as we forgive those who sin against us." Only as we forgive can we be forgiven.
f) The plea—"Lead us not into temptation."

II. THE PARABLE OF PRAYER—vv. 5-8

1. The problem—vv. 5-6. There was a need for bread. Do you have needs? God will meet them (Phil. 4:19).
2. The people—v. 7. Not willing to help. There are some who are so busy that they have no time to help others.
3. The persistence—v. 8. Because of the man's importunity (not willing to give up), the man would arise and give the bread that was needed.
   a) Daily prayer (James 5:16). Make it a daily habit to pray.
   b) Divine provision (John 15:7). Abiding in Christ.

III. THE PROMISES OF PRAYER—vv. 9-13

1. Simple promise—v. 9. Note: Ask, seek, knock. Praying need not be complicated. Even children can pray acceptably. Prayer does not depend on the language we use but on the attitude of our heart.
2. Sure promise—v. 10. Those who ask receive; those who seek find; and those who knock have the door opened. God will answer you when you pray.
3. Sincere promise—vv. 11-12. When the son asks for bread, does the father give him a stone? When he asks for an egg, does the father give a scorpion? If he asks for a fish, does he receive a serpent? God gives us what we ask for!
4. Steadfast promise—v. 13. If earthly fathers give good gifts to their children, then how much more shall God give good gifts to His children!

When you pray, don't give up! God will answer. His promises are true. God keeps His Word . . . He cannot lie (Num. 23:19). Call upon Him, and He will answer you (Jer. 33:3). For every promise in God's Word, we have a condition to meet. For example, before a person can be saved, he must confess his sin (I John 1:9). Make it a habit to pray. Prayer changes things, people, and situations.

19

PERSECUTION-PATIENCE-PERFECTION

Luke 13:1-17

These three words are very important to the Christian. Persecution comes to all those who follow Christ (II Tim. 3:12). All Christians need more patience. A Christian's patience should grow as he serves the Lord. God wants to heal His people. He wants to heal broken lives, spirits, bodies, and vows. He wants man to be whole.

I. THE PERSECUTION—vv. 1-5
   1. Persecution—v. 1. Pilate killed some Jews as they were making sacrifices at the temple in Jerusalem.
   2. Purpose—vv. 2-3. Were these people worse than other sinners? Why did they suffer? God treats all the same!
   3. Parable—vv. 4-5. When the tower of Siloam fell on eighteen people, did this mean they were worse sinners than others? Of course not. Note in verses 2-3 the importance of repentance!

II. THE PATIENCE—vv. 6-9
   1. Problem—v. 6. There is no fruit upon the fig tree. The master is angry (note the words of John 15:2).
   2. Plan—v. 7. The master wants to cut down the tree and destroy it since it has no fruit.
   3. Patience—vv. 8-9. The tree is given another chance—it is allowed to stand another year, before being destroyed.

III. THE PERFECTION—vv. 10-13
   1. Place—v. 10. Jesus is teaching in the synagogue on the sabbath. Though busy, He always had time for the house of God.
   2. Problem—v. 11. A woman who could not stand erect comes to Christ for healing. She had been in this condition for eighteen years!
   3. Perfection—v. 12. She is healed by Christ. He wants men to have healthy bodies as well as souls.
   4. Praise—v. 13. After being healed, the woman praises and glorifies the Lord.

IV. THE PROBLEM—vv. 14-17
   1. Reaction—v. 14. The ruler of the synagogue complains because Jesus has healed on the sabbath. These people never praised Christ for His good work. They always opposed Him for doing good. They were not sympathetic toward man's needs.

2. Reasoning—vv. 15-16. If an ox fell into a ditch on the sabbath, they would remove it, feeling they did no wrong. In this way they broke their own sabbath laws. Why shouldn't this woman, who had been sick for eighteen years, be healed on the sabbath?
3. Rejoicing—v. 17. Those accusing Christ become ashamed. The people rejoice at the healing.

The Jews were so concerned with their own man-made laws that they couldn't accept the good that Jesus did. These man-made laws had no feelings toward man and his need. These rulers were inconsistent—they did not keep their own laws. Laws are all right, if they agree with the Scriptures and show concern toward mankind.

20

RECEPTION AND REJECTION

Luke13:18-35

Some of the people who heard Christ preach accepted Him as Savior, the Messiah, the Son of God; others rejected Him. Many of the Jews surely knew the Old Testament Scriptures and the prophecies concerning Christ's coming and death, but their pride and self-righteousness kept them from accepting Christ as the Son of God.

I. THE PARABLES—vv. 18-21

1. Mustard seed parable—vv. 18-19. A mustard seed, which is very small, grows into a tree, and the birds lodge in it. So it is with the kingdom of God. It may have started small, but it grows larger than one can anticipate.
2. Measure of meal parable—vv. 20-21. The kingdom of God, like meal with yeast, rises and increases quickly. The growth of His kingdom knows no bounds.

II. THE PRETENSE—vv. 22-30

1. Savior—v. 22. Jesus goes from city to city, preaching and teaching, heading toward Jerusalem.
2. Salvation—v. 23. The people ask an important question: Who will be saved?
3. Strict—vv. 24-25. The door to heaven is narrow, and only a few

will enter (see Matt. 7:13-14). Some will knock, trying to get in, but they will hear these words, "I don't know you."

4. Sinful—vv. 26-27. These people were religious, but not righteous! The had a form of godliness, but no relationship with Christ. They could not enter (note the words of Jesus in Matt. 7:21-23). Only the born again (John 3:1-8) will enter.
5. Sorrow—v. 28. There will be weeping and gnashing of teeth. This means hell.
6. Satisfaction—vv. 29-30. People from all over the world will be in heaven. What great joy this will be!

III. THE PITY—vv. 31-35

1. Protection—v. 31. Jesus is warned to leave, because Herod was seeking Him, and planning to kill Him.
2. Plan—vv. 32-33. Jesus calls Herod a fox. A fox is cunning and destructive. Jesus would continue His work until His death. No one could destroy God's plan for man's salvation.
3. Pity—vv. 34-35. Sorrow fills the heart of Jesus. He is rejected. He foresees the destruction of Jerusalem.They will not see Him again until He comes into the city on Palm Sunday.

Those who believe and accept Christ will be saved; those who reject Him will be lost (Mark 16:16). All who believe in Him will have everlasting life (John 3:16). When man accepts Christ as His Savior, he becomes a son of God (John 1:12). Man has a twofold choice: (1) reception, or (2) rejection. No one can decide for another. It is a personal choice that must be made.

21

BEING HELPFUL

Luke 14:1-15

Man needs help! Without Christ man is not only helpless, but hopeless. God needs those who will help do His work. Before anyone can help with His work, they must be fitted for this service. Man must rely on Christ. His helpers must be humble, knowing that without the help of the Lord, they can do nothing. God works only through such people.

I. THE HEALING—vv. 1-6

1. Skeptics—vv. 1-2. The Jewish leaders and followers watch to see if Christ will heal the man with dropsy on the sabbath. They were always critical of Christ.
2. Silence—vv. 3-4. When the Jewish leaders do not respond to Christ's questions, He takes the sick man by the hand and leads him away.
3. Sabbath—v. 5. If an ox falls into the ditch on the sabbath, do you leave it there? Of course not! Then, why is it wrong to do good by healing the sick on the sabbath?
4. Speechless—v. 6. They cannot answer the Lord. Really, they had no just answer. By taking the ox out of the ditch on the sabbath, they were breaking their own man-made law. Why should they oppose Christ when He healed on the sabbath?

II. THE HUMILITY—vv. 7-11

1. Selfishness—vv. 7-8. Don't seek the best seats when asked to a party. Someone more important than you may be present and require your seat. Always think of others as better than yourself.
2. Shame—v. 9. An important person may come, and the host will give your seat to him. This would mean shame and embarrassment to you before the people.
3. Sincere—v. 10. Be yourself. Never seek to be above or better than others. Be humble and meek.
4. Spiritual—v. 11. Note the spiritual law here. If you exalt yourself, you will be humbled. If you humble yourself, you will be exalted.

III. THE HELPFULNESS—vv. 12-15

1. Plan—v. 12. When you have a dinner, don't invite your relatives and friends since they will invite you to their home for a meal later.
2. People—v. 13. Invite the poor, crippled, blind, and lame. Do it to help the people, expecting nothing in return.
3. Pleasure—vv. 14-15. Pleasure will be one result, but also at the judgment the Lord will reward you for your kindness.

We should never help people with the object that some day we may need help and they will owe us a favor. We should help people expecting nothing in return—not even a word of thanks. The good feeling that results from helping people should be ample pay and reward. However, God, who keeps good records, will reward us.

22
REPENTING BRINGS REJOICING
Luke 15:1-32

Jesus spoke often in parables. This lesson contains three parables. The parables Jesus gave were always:

1. Scriptural. He often quoted the Old Testament.
2. Spiritual. Each one had a spiritual truth for the hearer.
3. Sound. His parables always made sense.

I. THE LOST SHEEP—Luke 15:1-7

1. People—vv. 1-2. The publicans (tax collectors) and sinners came to hear Christ speak. The Pharisees were critical toward Him.
2. Parable—vv. 3-6.
   a) Sheep—vv. 3-4. If only one out of one hundred sheep were lost the shepherd would leave the ninety-nine to search for it.
   b) Satisfaction—vv. 5-6. Finding the lost sheep brings joy. All rejoice with the shepherd.
   c) Sinner—v. 7. When a sinner repents of his sin, the angels in heaven rejoice. Christ rejoices, and we should too.

We are as sheep gone astray (Isa. 53:5-6). Of all animals, a sheep is the only one who cannot find his way home. Christ came to die, and by this He could lead us home to heaven.

II. THE LOST SILVER—Luke 15:8-10

1. Remorse—v. 8. The lady lost a coin. This coin was worth seventeen cents, or a day's salary. The lady sought until she found it.
2. Rejoicing—v. 9. When she found the coin she rejoiced. Her neighbors rejoiced with her. We rejoice when a sinner finds Christ.
3. Repentance—v. 10. There is joy when a sinner repents of his sins and follows the Lord completely.

When a person works for the Lord and leads people to Christ, he has great joy. All sorrow and gloomy feelings leave when we tell others about Christ.

III. THE LOST SON—Luke 15:11-32

Here is a good picture of God the Father and the sinner.

1. Rebellion—vv. 12-13. The son wanted his share of the money. He left home and wasted his money on sinful living.
2. Results—vv. 14-16. His money gone—his friends gone! He fed the pigs. Even the pigs' food looked good. No one gave him food.

3. Realization—vv. 17-19. He thought of his home and father. He would arise and go to his father's home. He would repent of his wrong.
4. Return—vv. 20-21. The father forgave and gave his very best to him.
5. Rejoicing—vv. 22-24. There was rejoicing because of his return.
6. Rejection—vv. 25-32. The older brother didn't rejoice, but opposed the father's joy and the return of his brother. We should rejoice because our lost brother is found (note v. 32).

As Christians we should encourage new converts. We should not *push down,* but *lift up* these "babes in Christ." Don't be critical; be compassionate. Don't scold; encourage. Be interested in the problems of people. Rejoice with them when they rejoice and weep with them when they weep. Lack of love and patience with these people shows a lack of Christlikeness.

23

USING OUR MONEY PROPERLY

Luke 16:1-18

The sin most linked with pride in the Bible is greed, or the lust for worldly possessions. Loving money or possessions more than God is sin—and this sin is rampant in our world today. The more people get, the more they want—they are never satisfied. Rich people are fearful of losing what they have, so they have no joy. Poor people have less to lose, but instead of enjoying what they have they wish for the things they can't afford.

I. FAILURE CONDEMNED—Luke 16:1-3

1. Unjust steward—v. 1. The steward becomes careless. We, too, are stewards. All we have belongs to God. We are responsible to God for:
   a) Our time. We should use our time wisely (Ps. 90:12).
   b) Our talents. We must develop our God-given aptitudes (Eccles. 9:10).
   c) Our tithes. We owe this to God (Mal. 3:8-10).

d) Our traits. Our character and habits must be molded according to God's law (Gal. 5:22-23).
e) Our testimony. We must witness for Christ (I Cor. 9:27).

2. Undisciplined steward—vv. 2-3. The steward did not take good care of the Master's goods. His master called him to account for his actions. As Christians we should remember these three things as we live for God:
   a) Death is coming (Heb. 9:27).
   b) Christ is coming (John 14:1-3; Matt. 24:44).
   c) Judgment is coming (Rev. 20:11-15).

II. FORESIGHT COMMENDED—Luke 16:4-9

1. Steward's foresight—vv. 4-8. The steward used his position to decrease the amount of the poor people's debts to his master. The master praised the steward for his foresight. But it was wrong—the steward was really "buying friends" at his master's expense.
2. Sound foresight—vv. 8-9. We should use our money to advance the kingdom of God. Some people feel that their money will "buy their way into heaven."

Many people will spend thousands of dollars on their bodies, but spend no time on their souls, which will live forever!

III. FAITHFULNESS COUNSELED—Luke 16:10-18

1. Faithful in service—v. 10. The Christian must learn to be faithful in "small things." Note the importance of being faithful (Rev. 2:10; Matt. 24:13).
2. Faithful in substance—vv. 11-12. God wants our tithes and offerings. Our money belongs to God. *All* we have belongs to God!
3. Faithful servant—v. 13. Some people's god is money. They stay home from church on Sunday, but never from work on Monday. They miss church to visit friends, but never neglect their jobs to visit friends!
4. Foolishness seen—vv. 14-18. The religious leaders knew the way, but refused to accept it. They were foolish.

Christ's teaching was not popular in His day. Likewise, those who today preach His Word are not popular. All of God's true children face persecution and trouble. People who love money will despise: (1) self denial, (2) self discipline, and (3) self dedication. Put Christ *first* in your life!

24

HEAVEN AND HELL

Luke 16:19-31

There are only two places one can go after death—heaven or hell. We have a choice as to which place we will go. Some people say this is only a parable. However, in parables Jesus never mentioned the names of people. In this story He did! Jesus taught more about hell than about heaven. Look at some of the Scriptures about hell. (1) The wicked shall be turned into hell (Ps. 9:17). (2) Punishment is everlasting (Dan. 12:2). (3) The people who will be in hell are described (Rev. 21:8). There will be no rest in hell (Rev. 14:11, 20:10). There are many more.

I. THE PERSONS—vv. 19-21

1. Man of wealth—v. 19. "There was a certain rich man," Jesus said, "who was splendidly clothed and lived each day in mirth and luxury" (LB). Sometimes he is called "Dives," the Latin word for "rich."
2. Man of want—v. 20-21 "One day Lazarus, a diseased beggar, was laid at his door. As he lay there longing for scraps from the rich man's table, the dogs would come and lick his open sores" (LB).

II. THE PARTICULARS—vv. 22-26

1. Heaven—v. 22. "Finally the beggar died and was carried by the angels to be with Abraham in the place of the righteous dead. The rich man also died and was buried" (LB).
2. Hell—v. 23. "And his soul went to hell. There, in torment, he saw Lazarus in the far distance with Abraham" (LB).
3. Help—v. 24. The rich man cries out for water to cool his tongue, because he is tormented in hell.
4. Helpless—v. 25. It is too late to change now. He had had the opportunity while he was alive; after death it is too late (Heb. 9:27).
5. Horror—v. 26. Once a person enters hell, they never get out! The rich man did not go to hell because of his riches, but because he lived for himself and not for God.

III. THE PLEA—vv. 27-31

1. The Plain—vv. 27-28. "Then the rich man said, 'O Father Abraham, then please send him to my father's home—For I have five brothers—to warn them about this place of torment lest they

come here when they die' " (LB; compare with Rev. 20:10; 14:11).

2. The Prophets—v. 29. "But Abraham said, 'The Scriptures have warned them again and again. Your brothers can read them any time they want to" (LB). There is no excuse for man to be lost.
3. The Proposal—v. 30. The rich man thought if someone arose from the dead and went back to earth, then his brothers would believe and repent of their sins.
4. The Problem—v. 31. If the brothers did not believe Moses and the other prophets, neither would they believe if someone arose from the dead and went to them. The Pharisees did not believe Jesus when He arose from the dead.

Besides a real hell, there is also a real heaven. Notice some of the verses from the Bible: (1) The words of Jesus (John 14:1-6). (2) Second Corinthians 5:1 tells of a home not made with human hands. (3) Abraham looked for a city made by God (Heb. 11:10). (4) Paul told of being with Christ after death—(II Cor. 5:8). (5) The Bible tells of the new heaven (Rev. 22:1-7). There are only two places—heaven and hell. Which place will *you* be after you die? What you do with Christ decides where you will be!

25

SIN AND FORGIVENESS

Luke 17:1-10

Sin brings shame. It brings shame to the person committing it. It brings shame to that person's family and friends. In some cases, it brings shame to a community, and even to a nation. Christians should oppose sin. If Christians fought sin with more zeal there would be less sin.

I. THE FALLING—vv. 1-2
1. Sin's power—v. 1. There will always be sin and temptation. However, when you cause others to sin by encouraging or tempting them, judgment awaits.
2. Sin's punishment—v. 2. It would be better for him to die than to face the judgment for causing others to sin.

II. THE FORGIVENESS—vv. 3-4

1. Self—v. 3. "Take heed to yourselves"—be careful how you live.
2. Sin—v. 3. "If thy brother trespass against thee, restore him." Hate sin, but love the sinner. Rebuke sinners in love.
3. Sincere—v. 3. "If he repents, forgive him."
4. Surrender—v. 4. Forgive those who wrong you seven times a day, and if they wrong you over seven times daily, continue to forgive them.

III. THE FAITH—vv. 5-6

1. Increase of faith—v. 5. The disciples request an increase in their faith. We may increase our faith by reading God's Word daily (Rom. 10:17). Read Hebrews 11 to see the great accomplishments by men of God who had great faith.
2. Influence of faith—v. 6. Those with faith the size of a mustard seed could curse a tree and it would be planted in the sea. There is great power in faith. It is necessary to have faith in order to please God (Heb. 11:6).

IV. THE FAITHFULNESS—vv. 7-10

1. Symbol—vv. 7-9. The servant, though he works hard in the field, still prepared the meal for his master. We too must remember that Christ is first in our lives (Matt. 6:33).
2. Savior—v. 10. If we do anything for the Lord as a duty, we will lose our reward. Whatever we do for the Lord, we should do because we love Him. A religion that causes man to do things as a duty is an empty, dead religion.

God wants man to be faithful to His Word and His Son. When he is faithful, he brings honor and glory to God. He also makes an impact on others.

Those who commit sin by habit are servants, or slaves, to sin (John 8:34). Satan is their master. Christians do good things because of their love for the Lord. It is not a duty or responsibility—it is a privilege. It is a joy to serve the Lord and to do His work.

26

CHRISTIAN GRATITUDE

Luke 17:11-19

Man is quick to express his needs to the Lord, but very slow to give thanks. As a Christian, think for a moment and ask yourself this question: "How often do I thank the Lord?" Then think of how often you ask the Lord in prayer to help you to meet your needs, and to be with you. It shows a lack of respect when we fail to thank God for His blessings.

I. THE PEOPLE—vv. 11-13
   1. Christ—v. 11. Luke shows to us the last six months of Christ's ministry as one long journey to Jerusalem and the cross.
   2. Characters—v. 12. Lepers. Lepers were outcasts. They were unclean. They were separated from family and friends. They were helpless. This sickness starts as a skin disease, then the fingers and hands, and feet are affected and fall off at the joints. SIN IS LIKE THIS DISEASE BECAUSE:
      a) It separates (Ps. 66:18). Sin separates from God.
      b) It makes one unclean (John 3:1-8). Because of sin, man must be born again. He must be changed by God's power.
      c) There is no cure aside from God's intervention (Heb. 9:22).
   3. Cry—v. 13. The lepers cry out for help. No one seemed to care. No one seemed interested.

II. THE PLAN—v. 14
   1. Command—v. 14a. "And when he saw them he said unto them, Go shew yourselves unto the priests."
      a) Permission. If they were cured, the lepers would be given permission to appear in public.
      b) Purity—The priests would give the final decision regarding healing and purity.
   2. Cleansed—v. 14b. "And it came to pass, that, as they went, they were cleansed." Obedience always brings results.
      a) Obedience brings cleansing. The lepers had to obey and *go* before they were cleansed.
      b) Obedience shows consecration. A consecrated person will be quick to obey what the Lord commands.

III. THE PRAISE—vv. 15-19
   1. Happiness—v. 15. Only one of the ten lepers returned to give thanks. No doubt all the lepers were happy and thankful, but only

one showed thanks. He returned to thank Jesus before he went to the priest.

2. Humility—v. 16. He was a Samaritan, and bowing before Christ, who was a Jew, showed real humility, for the Jews and Samaritans did not get along with each other.
3. Healing—vv. 17-19
   a) People—v. 17. Christ healed ten—where were the nine?
   b) Problem—v. 18. Only one was thankful. What a shame!
   c) Power—v. 19. Jesus said, "Thy faith hath made thee whole."

The Bible says, "In everything give thanks" (I Thess. 5:18). Be thankful for these things: (1) Problems—they help you. (2) People—all the people who have helped you. (3) Pastor—because he explains God's Word to you. (4) Persecution—it makes you grow in the Lord. (5) The opportunity to pray—when Daniel prayed, he also gave thanks (Dan. 6:10). Thanksgiving gives joy and peace.

27
CHRIST'S COMING
Luke 17:20-37

Jesus will come again! He will come soon. When comparing what's happening in the world today with the Bible, we see that His coming is drawing nearer. Some Christians are so busy that they don't realize that His coming is near. Here are some things which keep people from looking for His coming:

(1) Self. Making plans, achieving ambitions, fulfilling desires, and obtaining possessions.
(2) Sin. Loving pleasure and worldly things more than God.
(3) Sloth. Being lazy, indifferent, and unconcerned about the things of the spirit.
(4) Satan. He tells people, "You have plenty of time before Christ comes."

I. THE PROPHECY—vv. 20-25

1. Signs—vv. 20-21. "One day the Pharisees asked Jesus, 'When will the kingdom of God begin.' Jesus replied, 'The Kingdom of God isn't ushered in with visible signs. You won't be able to say,

"It has begun here in this place or there in that part of the country." For the kingdom of God is within you' " (LB).

2. Shame—v. 23. Some people will say, "Christ has already come." Do not believe them!
3. Surety—v. 24. When He comes, we will see Him, just as we see the lightning flash across the sky. It will also occur as quickly as a lightning flash.
4. Suffering—v. 25. People will reject Christ and He will suffer (compare with John 1:11-12). Christ is rejected not only by the Jews. He has been rejected by many Protestants and Catholics also.

II. THE PEOPLE—vv. 26-32

1. People—v. 26. Christ's coming will occur in the same manner as the Flood of Noah's day.
2. Particulars—v. 27. Compare with Genesis 6—8
   a) Eating. Today many people's idol is their belly.
   b) Drinking. More than twenty-five thousand are killed yearly by drunken drivers. Children are hungry, and there are many divorces because of drinking!
   c) Marrying. This really means looseness in marriage, divorces, and immorality. We have over 800,000 divorces yearly in the USA. The people in Genesis 6—8 refused to listen, and didn't know what happened until the Flood came. Satan had blinded them to the truth.
3. Perversion—vv. 28-30. They were guilty of the sins listed in Romans 1:26-27. People who commit these sins cannot enter heaven (I Cor. 6:9). God gives them up! This is one of the fastest growing sins today.
4. Possessions—vv. 31-32. Having your mind upon possessions. Note verse 32, "Remember Lot's wife." Her heart and mind was in Sodom.

III. THE PREPARATION—vv. 33-37

1. Preparation—v. 33. Losing your life—that is, giving it to Christ; or saving your life—that is, using it for selfish desires and plans.
2. People—vv. 34-36
   a) Sleeping—v. 34. Two are asleep—one is taken, the other is left.
   b) Working—vv. 35-36. Two men, two women, one is taken and the other is left.

3. Problem—v. 37. God's judgment will fall on those not ready, like vultures fly down on dead animals.

As Christians, we should always be looking for His coming. However, we should not be so busy looking for His coming that we have no time to be busy working for Him. Remember, every person that is not ready for His coming will be lost and separated from God. This means they will go to hell. Let's be busy in warning people about Christ's coming.

28

PERSISTENCE-PRIDE-PARDON

Luke 18:1-17

Jesus speaks about three things in this passage of Scripture. (1) Persistence—all Christians must be persistent in their living, or they will be a failure in the Christian life. (2) Pride—Christ speaks of selfish, spiritual pride, which keeps many people away from God. (3) Pardon—those who are sincere toward God will find pardon from their sins. No sin is too great. No one is too great a sinner to receive this pardon.

I. SINCERE PERSISTENCE—vv. 1-8
1. Prayer—v. 1. Man should always pray and not faint (compare I Thess. 5:17).
2. People—vv. 2-3. A judge, who feared neither God nor man. A widow, who came again and again, seeking justice.
3. Persistence—vv. 4-5. The judge ignored her plea for a long time, but because of her persistence he finally meted out justice. It was her continual coming to the judge that caused him to give her the desires of her heart.
4. Picture—vv. 6-8. If the ungodly judge gave the woman justice because of her constant pleas, how much more will a just God hear and answer our prayers (compare James 5:16; Jer. 33:3; Matt. 7:7-9).

II. SINFUL PRIDE—vv. 9-14
1. Parable—v. 9. A parable of a publican and a Pharisee is used by Jesus to explain a truth.

2. People—v. 10. The Pharisee and the publican both go to the temple to pray.
3. Pharisee's prayer—vv. 11-12. His prayer is filled with boasting and self-righteousness. The personal pronoun *I* is mentioned five times.
4. Publican's prayer—v. 13. His prayer is simple, without any boasting. "God be merciful to me a sinner."
5. Pride—v. 14. God answers the publican's prayer, not the prayer of the Pharisee. Note: If a person exalts himself, he will be humbled . . . if he humbles himself, he will be exalted (see Matt. 23:12).

III. SIMPLE PARDON—vv. 15-17
1. Bringing children—v. 15. Children are brought to Jesus to be blessed. The disciples rebuke those bringing them, claiming that Christ has no time for them.
2. Blessing the children—v. 16. Jesus accepts the children and blesses them. He then says that of such is the kingdom of God. In simple words, His kingdom is simple enough for children to accept.
3. Becoming as children—v. 17. We must be converted, and become as children if we expect to enter heaven.

Pride separates men from God—both now on earth and, later, in eternity. Satan uses pride to destroy many people. Be humble before God. Learn to crucify yourself, putting the Lord first in your plans and ambitions.

29

SALVATION AND HEALING

Luke 18:18-43

Christ came to help man both spiritually and physically. He wants man to have a healthy soul and body. Christ brings divine health. By accepting Christ, we have a healthy soul. By God's touch, we have a healthy body.

I. SALVATION—vv. 18-27
1. Concern—v. 18. What must I do that I may have eternal life?

2. Christ—v. 19. Jesus says, Don't call me good . . . there is only one who is good! What humility!
3. Commandments—vv. 20-21. Five commandments are listed and he claimed he had kept them from his youth. (He didn't keep the first commandment, which puts God first in one's life.)
4. Consecration—vv. 22-23. Jesus asks three things of the ruler: (1) Sell what you have. (2) Give your riches to the poor. (3) Take up your cross daily and follow Me. The questioner goes away filled with sorrow.
5. Comparison—vv. 24-25. It is hard for rich people to enter heaven since money comes between man and God. Christ must be first!
6. Christian—vv. 26-27. Who can be saved? With man things are impossible. With God, all things are possible.

II. SACRIFICE—vv. 28-30
1. Consecration—v. 28. Leave all to follow Christ.
2. Compensation—vv. 29-30. He who leaves all and follows Christ will be rewarded, both in this life and in the life to come. God keeps very good records.

III. SORROW—vv. 31-34
1. Prophecy—v. 31. Jesus now faces the end of His life. He knows the prophecies which point to His death, and how they must be fulfilled.
2. Punishment—vv. 32-33. Suffering, death upon the cross, and the resurrection now await Him.
3. Problem—v. 34. The disciples, although with Him for three years, do not understand the words of Christ.

IV. SEARCHING—vv. 35-43
1. Person—vv. 35-37. A blind man hears that Jesus is coming to his town.
2. Pleading—v. 38. He cries out to Christ, asking that He heal his blindness.
3. Problems—v. 39. He is told by the crowd to keep silent.
4. Personal—vv. 40-41. Jesus takes a personal interest—He stands still. He asks the blind man what he wants.
5. Praise—vv. 42-43. The blind man is healed. He praises God, along with the other people.

As Jesus "stood still" for this blind man, so He stops to listen to our needs. He could have passed this blind man and shown no interest. But He is concerned and interested in all of man's needs.

30
CHRIST THE KING
Luke 19:28-44

Christ knew the future. He knew He was entering Jerusalem for the last time. He knew death was near. Despite this, He did not shrink back from "going all the way" for the sins of man. As Christ rides into the city, He is made king. He was born to be king. He wants to be king in the hearts of all men.

I. THE PREPARATION—vv. 28-35
  1. Plan—v. 28. Jesus knew the plan of God for His life. He goes ahead, leading the people into Jerusalem.
  2. Place—v. 29. Bethphage, less than a mile from Jerusalem. Bethany was about two miles from Jerusalem.
  3. Purpose—vv. 30-31. Go and get a small colt that never had been ridden before. Only animals like this could be used for something sacred (Num. 19:2; Deut. 21:3).
  4. People—32-35
     a) Disciples—v. 32. The two disciples obey.
     b) Demand—v. 33. The owners ask why they are taking the donkey.
     c) Divinity—vv. 34-35. The Lord needed the donkey.

II. THE PRAISE—vv. 36-40
  1. People—v. 36. The people spread their clothes on the donkey. Some lay their clothes along the way for Him to ride over.
  2. Praise—v. 37. The people rejoice and praise the Lord. They are impressed with the Lord, who earlier had raised Lazarus from the dead.
  3. Peace—v. 38. The people bless the Lord. "Peace in heaven" means accepting Christ as "the Prince of Peace."
  4. Problem—vv. 39-40. The Pharisees want Christ to calm the disciples. Note the words of Christ in verse 40. If people don't praise the Lord, then the stones will cry out in praise to God.

III. THE PROPHECY—vv. 41-44
  1. Sorrow—v. 41. As Christ comes near to Jerusalem, He weeps over the city. He weeps not only because the people had rejected Him, but because they had rejected God by rejecting Christ.
  2. Shame—v. 42. "Eternal peace was within your reach and you turned it down," He wept, "and now it is too late " (LB). People

can have peace, if they only accept Christ as Savior. If they only give Him a place in their lives.

3. Sadness—vv. 43-44. "Your enemies will pile up earth against your walls and encircle you and close in on you, and crush you to the ground, and your children within you; your enemies will not leave one stone upon another—for you have rejected the opportunity God offered you" (LB).

Just as Christ was made king in Jerusalem, He wants to be made "king in our lives." He does not force Himself into our hearts. He stands, knocking at our heart's door (Rev. 3:20). There is a danger after He enters our heart that we become so busy with other things that He is crowded out. Allow Him to have full control of your heart and life. Let Him not only be your Savior, but your king as well.

31

WISDOM OF CHRIST

Luke 20:1-26

Jesus was the Son of Man, but also the Son of God. Being the Son of God, He had divine wisdom. His enemies sought ways of trapping Him, trying to confuse and destroy Him. However, His answers always silenced His enemies. All types of tricks and schemes were used, but all of them failed.

I. THE AUTHORITY—vv. 1-8

1. Request—vv. 1-2. As Jesus is preaching the gospel in the temple, He is asked by the Jewish leaders where He received His authority to teach and do many things. (Keep in mind, the Jews didn't want to accept Him as the Messiah.)
2. Reaction—vv. 3-4. Jesus responds with a question. He asks, Was John sent by God, or was he on his own?
3. Reasoning—vv. 5-7. The Jews reason among themselves. If John was from God, why didn't you accept him? If not of God, the people would have stoned them. They had no answer.
4. Response—v. 8. Jesus' response—"Neither tell I you by what authority I do these things."

II. THE ALLEGORY—vv. 9-18

1. Parable—vv. 5-12. Man and his vineyard. When ready to reap the harvest, the husbandman was beaten. Two different servants were sent, and both received the same treatment.
2. Plan—v. 13. The owner said, I will send my son, and they will respect him.
3. Plot—vv. 14-15. They make plans to kill the owner's son, which they did, showing no respect to the owner or his son.
4. Punishment—v. 16. The owner will surely punish these people for their deeds.
5. Picture—vv. 17-18. God sent the prophets to warn the people. They mistreated and killed them. Jesus, the Chief Cornerstone, is rejected. If we humble ourselves before Christ, we will be saved. If we reject Him we will be crushed to death.

III. THE ALLEGIANCE—vv. 19-26

1. Plot—vv. 19-20. The Jews want to destroy Christ, so they wait for something He may say which can be held against Him and used by the government to destroy Him.
2. Plan—vv. 21-25. They try to trick Jesus in allegiance to God or government. Jesus uses a coin, and simply says, Give to the emperor what is due him, and to God what is due Him.
3. Power—v. 26. Their plan to outwit him has failed. The people marvel at His wisdom and power.

Even today, people seek faults with God's work and church. They seek and excuse for not serving God.

God wants our allegiance; but He also wants us to be loyal to country and community. God expects His children to be good citizens. We must keep not only God's laws, but man's laws as well. Herein is a good example for God's people to set—full obedience to God and man as well.

32

RESURRECTION AND RELIGION

Luke 20:27-47

There will be a resurrection for God's people. There will also be a resurrection for the sinner. Many are interested as to what will happen in the resurrection. The Bible tells us some details, although many things are not told. Christians should not be as concerned about the future as they are about the present.

I. THE RESURRECTION—vv. 27-38
   1. Resurrection—v. 27. Jesus is questioned as to what will happen after the resurrection.
   2. Reunited—vv. 28-33. If a woman's husband dies and she is remarried six times, which of the seven men will be her husband in heaven?
   3. Reasoning—vv. 34-36. Jesus reasons with the people, saying in heaven there will be no marriage. There will be no husband/wife relationship. We will be as the angels.
   4. Rejoicing—vv. 37-38. There will be life after death. For the Christian, eternal life. For the sinner, it will be eternal *doom*—eternal separation from God.

II. REASONING—vv. 39-44
   1. Answers—vv. 39-40. Jesus had answered their questions so well that some are fearful to ask Him any more, lest they be humiliated like those in the past.
   2. Asking—vv. 41-44. They ask questions concerning David and how Christ came through him. They also ask about why Jesus is called the son of David. They knew the answers to this. They become technical, seeking to find some flaw or mistake in Christ's answers.

   Man today still seeks technical questions, looking for some flaw or reason why they should not live for God and serve Him. Most of these people know the truth but are not willing to accept it.

III. RELIGIOUS—vv. 45-47
   1. Warning—vv. 45-46. "Then, with the crowds listening, he turned to his disciples and said, 'Beware of these experts in religion, for they love to parade in dignified robes and to be bowed to by the people as they walk along the street. And how they love the seats of honor in the synagogues and at religious festivals!' " (LB).
   2. Wrong—v. 47. While they act so spiritual, they continue to cheat the widows of their property. In simple words, they live a hypocritical life. They had an outward appearance of religion, but their hearts were far from God.

The Bible teaches that hypocrites will be lost. They will not be in heaven! The Pharisees were very religious, but their hearts were far from God. They had an outward appearance of religion, but they were not righteous. The righteous man lives differently from the world (II Cor. 5:17). He has been changed by the power of God. He follows the teachings of the Bible.

33
CHRIST'S COMING

Luke 21:1-38

Here we see some of the details of the coming of Christ. He gives a list of the things which will happen before He returns. God doesn't want us to be ignorant concerning His coming. Compare this passage to Matthew 24, and II Timothy 3:1-5. Then, compare it with your daily newspapers, which show that we are living in the last days, just before the Lord returns. His return could occur at any time.

I. CHRISTIAN CONTRIBUTION—vv. 1-4

1. Giving—vv. 1-2. Two types of giving: (1) the rich, (2) the widow. She gave two mites—two copper coins.
2. Gifts—vv. 3-5. Percentage wise, the woman gave more than the rich gave.

In giving, it is not how much we give, but what we are unwilling to give. It is not what we give, but what we have left.

II. CHRIST'S COMING—vv. 5-31

1. Symbol—vv. 5-7. Jesus used the temple as an example of what will happen when He returns. The disciples ask when this great event will take place.
2. Signs—vv. 8-31.
   a) First group of signs—vv. 8-11. Note these signs: Deception, wars, earthquakes, famines, signs in the heavens. Look around today, and you see these being fulfilled.
   b) Second group of signs—vv. 12-19. Christians will be persecuted, betrayed, and hated. The antichrist forces are at work today, creating bad feeling toward Christians.
   c) Third group of signs—vv. 20-24. Military might will increase. Many will be killed, until the time of the Gentiles be fulfilled. All nations will increase their military might.

d) Fourth group of signs—vv. 25-28. Signs in the heavens. Time of distress of nations. Men's hearts will fail them for fear. The Son of God will come.

e) Fifth sign—vv. 29-31. Sign of the fig tree. When you see the above events happen, you know the end is near!

III. CHRIST'S CONCERN—vv. 32-38

1. Surety—vv. 32-33. All these events will take place within a generation (note v. 33, showing God's Word to be true).
2. Slothfulness—vv. 34-35. Be careful of these three sins: surfeiting, drunkenness, and being submerged by cares of this life.
3. Salvation—v. 36. Live so that you are ready for His coming, and thus escape the tribulation.
4. Savior—vv. 37-38. People come to hear Him teach. He goes to the Mount of Olives—perhaps to pray for strength.

The signs of Christ's return are all around us. However, knowing all the signs is not sufficient—we must be ready to meet Him. A person is ready only when Christ lives within his heart. His coming is near—be ready to meet Him. His coming will be unexpected. It will be quick. Now is the time to prepare.

34
THE PASSOVER
Luke 22:1-38

Jesus would keep the Passover Feast with His disciples. It would be His last meal with them. He knew He was facing the cross and soon He would die for the sins of man. He relates some of the events concerning His death.

I. THE PASSOVER—vv. 1-6

1. Passover—vv. 1-2. The Passover is near. The Jewish leaders are plotting ways of destroying Christ.
2. Plot—vv. 3-6. Satan will work through Judas, one of the twelve disciples who have been with Christ for three years.

II. THE PREPARATION—vv. 7-13

1. Remembrance—vv. 7-8. Jesus will observe this Passover Feast with His disciples.

2. Room—vv. 9-13. Jesus informs the disciples where to find the proper room. They obey His instructions and make preparation.

III. THE PARTICULARS—vv. 14-23

1. Passover—vv. 14-16. This would be the last meal with His disciples—their last close contact.
2. Particulars—vv. 17-19. The bread is a symbol of His body and the wine of His blood.
3. Promise—vv. 20-21. His blood, the forgiveness of man's sin (compare Heb. 9:22; I John 1:7).
4. Pity—vv. 22-23. Woe unto the man that will betray Him. The disciples wonder, who is this person?

IV. THE PRIDE—vv. 24-30

1. Selfishness—v. 24. Disciples wonder who will be greatest in the kingdom of God.
2. Symbol—vv. 25-30. A master appoints his slaves; just so Christ will appoint the disciples to their proper place.

V. THE PROBLEM—vv. 31-34

1. Plan—vv. 31-32. Satan will use Peter wrongly to tempt Christ.
2. Pride—v. 33. Peter boasts of his loyalty to Christ.
3. Problem—v. 34. Peter will deny Christ three times.

VI. THE PREACHING—vv. 35-38

1. Preach—v. 35. Jesus sends His disciples out to preach. They are to preach the gospel—no social work.
2. Prophecy—vv. 36-37. The prophecy of Christ's death will soon come true.
3. Provision—v. 38. Their provision is sufficient.

Christ paid the price for man's salvation on the cross. This death brought hope for salvation for all mankind. All man needs do is to accept Christ as Savior. By doing this, man is fit for heaven. His sins are gone. At death he will go to the Lord in heaven and live with Him eternally.

35

THE PRAYING SAVIOR

Luke 22:39-46

Christ was a "man of prayer." His prayers in public were always short! His private prayers were long. In fact, sometimes He prayed all night. The prayer by which Lazarus was brought back from the dead was composed of just fifty-two words (John 11:41-43). Though Christ was divine, He was also human. He became weary and tired. Yet He always sought God for help and strength. He not only prayed, but taught us to pray (Luke 18:1; 11:1; Matt. 6:6; 7:7-9).

I. THE ATTENTION—vv. 39-40

1. Practice—v. 39. He often went to the Mount of Olives. Here He spent time alone in prayer. He taught the importance of secret praying (Matt. 6:6).
2. Prayer—v. 40. Prayer strengthens us to face and overcome temptations. Don't wait to pray until you are tempted. Pray now. Prepare yourself. Note these words, "He told them. 'Pray God that you will not be overcome by temptation" (LB).

II. THE ATTITUDE—vv. 41-42

1. Respect—v. 41. Note that Jesus kneeled. Kneeling shows a reverence and respect for God.
2. Request—v. 42. Remove the cup! The cup was a symbol of suffering. In this cup was all the agony and suffering of the cross. In other words, Jesus was saying, "If it is possible to forgive man of his sin another way than by my death, then do it." Remember that Jesus had human feelings. He didn't like suffering and persecution.

III. THE ANGELS—v. 43

The angels ministered unto the Lord.

1. Person of angels. They are heavenly beings. They defend us, fighting against the power of Satan (Jude 9).
2. Protection of angels (Ps. 91:11-12). Notice that angels protect us. Though we may not see them, they are round about us.
3. Power of angels. The angels strengthen Jesus (Matt. 4:11). Angels freed Lot and his wife from Sodom (Gen. 19:1-26).

IV. THE AGONY—v. 44

1. Suffering—"And being in agony." He had all the sins of the world upon Him as He died for His enemies (Rom. 5:8).

2. Sincere—"He prayed more earnestly." He was sincere. He was deeply concerned. His love was without limit (John 15:15).
3. Sweat—"And his sweat was as it were great drops of blood falling down to the ground." Under great strain, people have been known to sweat blood. He knew the agony that He confronted, predicted in Isaiah 53.

V. THE ADVICE—vv. 45-56
1. Asleep—v. 45. The disciples become weary and go to sleep. (Samson was sleeping when he lost his strength, symbolized by his long hair [Judg. 16:19-20].)
2. Advice—v. 46. Jesus is really saying, "Begin now to pray and prepare yourself. Then, when temptation comes, you will be victorious." He gives power for each temptation (I Cor. 10:13).

Christ's ministry started with prayer (Matt. 4:1-11). His whole life was filled with prayer. His life ended with prayer (Luke 23:34). All great men of the Bible were men who prayed. Prayer changes things, but prayer also changes *people!* If you pray every day, you will not remain the same person.

36
DECIDING ABOUT CHRIST
Luke 23:1-25

Jesus enters the city, is arrested, then faces trial. The people in Jerusalem are determined to destroy Christ. The Sanhedrin (Jewish high court) pronounces the death penalty on Jesus. The Romans try Him, and they too want to kill Christ. Pilate was the same age as Jesus. In the beginning he did not get along too well with the Jews. During A.D. 36, seven years after the death of Christ, Pilate committed suicide.

I. THE PEOPLE—Luke 23:1-5
1. Arrest—v 1. Christ is brought before the governor, Pilate.
2. Accusing—v. 2. They accuse Christ of things which were not true. Christ, the perfect Son of God did no wrong, so His enemies had to make up false charges
3. Answer—v. 3. Pilate asks Christ, "Are you King of the Jews?" To this question, Jesus answers Yes!

4. Effect—v. 4. Pilate says, "I find no fault in this man." There were no real charges against Christ—just lies and false accusations.
5. Attitude—v. 5. "Then they became desperate. 'But he is causing riots against the government everywhere He goes, all over Judea, from Galilee to Jerusalem' " (LB).

II. THE PERSECUTION—Luke 23:6-12

1. Transferred—vv. 6-7. Pilate turns the case over to Herod. This is the same Herod who beheaded John the Baptist. Herod was curious to see Jesus. He thought Jesus was John the Baptist risen from the dead.
2. Trial—vv. 8-9. Herod wanted Christ to perform a miracle and to "show off" His power. Jesus did not answer Herod.
3. Testimony—v. 10. The chief priest and religious leaders accused Christ of false charges.
4. Testing—vv. 11-12. They mocked Christ as KING OF THE JEWS! Perhaps they were testing the patience of Christ . . . they knew His teaching about love, forgiveness, and patience (note v. 12). Herod and Pilate had been enemies but now were friends. Pilate makes Herod feel important by turning the decision over to him.

III. THE PLAN—Luke 23:13-25

The Jews had one plan—to destroy Christ!

1. Perfect—vv. 13-14. Pilate found no wrong or fault in Christ.
2. Penalty—v. 15. How could they punish Christ? He had done nothing wrong.
3. Punishment—v. 16. Pilate will chastise Christ (whip him thirty-nine-times), then let Him go free.
4. People—vv. 17-19. "But now a mighty roar rose from the crowd as with one voice they shouted, 'Kill him, and release Barabbas to us.' (Barabbas was in prison for starting an insurrection in Jerusalem against the government, and for murder' " [LB]).
5. Plan—vv. 20-21. Pilate tries to free Christ; the people resist.
6. Prevailing—vv. 22-23. The *people's voices* are louder than the *conscience of Pilate*.
7. Problem—vv. 24-25. A murderer is set free; Christ is sentenced to die.

Who was responsible for Christ's death? The Jews? The Romans? *All* of us were responsible (Isa. 53:5-6). He was nailed to the cross *for you*, for *me*. Our sins helped nail Christ to the cross.

37

DEATH OF THE SAVIOR

Luke 23:26-56

Looking at the cross will change us. It draws us closer to the Lord. Note the words, "Who gave Himself for *me*" (Gal. 2:20).

I. THE PROPHECY—vv. 26-31
1. Person—v. 26. Simon the Cyrenian bore the cross for Christ.
2. People—v. 27. Large crowds followed Christ to the cross.
3. Prophecy—vv. 28-31. Jesus speaks of the tribulation, which will take place after He returns at the Rapture.

II. THE PUNISHMENT—vv. 32-38
1. Criminals—vv. 32-33. Two criminals are crucified for their sins. Jesus, without sin, dies for the sins of all people.
2. Concern—v. 34a. Christ forgives those who crucify Him.
3. Clothing—v. 34b. The soldiers gamble for His clothing.
4. Criticism—v. 35. He could have saved Himself but refused.
5. Complete—vv. 36-37. He refuses to accept anything for the pain.
6. Christ—v. 38. The people admit He was the Son of God. Message written in three languages so all could understand.

III. THE PARDON—vv. 39-43
1. Skeptic—doubt, vv. 39-41. "If thou be the Son of God . . ." The other thief rebukes him because they are justly dying for their sins.
2. Sincere—faith, v. 42. The cry, "Remember me." He also calls Christ, "Lord." He has respect for Him. He accepts Him.
3. Savior—pardon v. 43. On the cross, He forgives the criminal, who had simple faith in His words.

IV. THE PARTING—vv.44-49
1. Darkness—vv. 44-45. Even nature has respect for Christ. The sun refuses to shine. There is darkness in the afternoon.
2. Death—v. 46. Note, Jesus cries with a loud voice. He does not die a weak death; He dies a strong man.
3. Divine—vv. 47-49. The centurion acknowledges Christ as a righteous man. The people recognize Jesus as the Son of God.

V. THE PREPARATION—vv. 50-56
1. Person—vv. 50-51. Joseph asks Sandhedrin court for His body.
2. Place—v. 52. He would place Christ's body in his own tomb.

3. Poverty—v. 53. Jesus buried in a borrowed tomb. Born in a stable. What humility!
4. Preparation—v. 54. The sabbath began Friday at 6:00 P.M. and lasted until 6:00 P.M. Saturday.
5. Plans—vv. 55-56. The women prepare spices, perfumes, salves, and oil to anoint the body of Christ.

Christ fulfilled all the Old Testment prophecies. He paid the full price. He took man's hell upon the cross. He lived a perfect life. He died an atoning death, and rose from the dead as a token of His completed sacrifice for the sin of mankind.

38
THE RESURRECTION
Luke 24:1-29

Christ arose from the dead, both body and soul. After He arose, He appeared to the eleven disciples (Luke 24:45). He appeared to various groups after His resurrection. Forty days later, He ascended into heaven, and is now seated on the right hand of God.

I. THE PEOPLE—vv. 1-7
1. People—v. 1. The women come to the tomb before dawn.
2. Power—vv. 2-3. The grave is empty. The best Christian testimony is the empty cross and the empty tomb.
3. Perplexed—v. 4. The women are confused. Has someone stolen the body of Christ?
4. Problem—v. 5. Why are you seeking Christ? He is not here, He is risen as He said.
5. Promise—vv. 6-7. If they destroyed His temple (body) the Lord would raise Him up in three days (see John 2:19-22).

II. THE POWER—vv. 8-12
1. Remembrance—v. 8. They now remember His words, telling how He would rise from the dead.
2. Returning—vv. 9-10. They return to the city, spreading the good news.
3. Rejection—v. 11. Some reject the good news. Even the disciples were doubtful.

4. Reality—v. 12. Peter runs to the tomb, looks in. He had to see for himself.

III. THE PERSON—vv. 13-24

1. People—vv. 13-16. Two disciples walk along the road to Emmaus. They talk about the resurrection.
2. Problems—vv. 17-19. The two disciples, one Cleopas, the other perhaps Luke, do not recognize Jesus as He walks with them, and they share with Him the news of the resurrection.
3. Person—vv. 20-21. They tell all about Jesus, His miracles, and His teaching and that they had hoped He was the Messiah.
4. Power—vv. 22-24. They tell how Christ had resurrection power.

IV. THE PROPHECY—vv. 25-29

1. People—vv. 25-26. Jesus scolds them for not accepting and believing the Old Testament prophecies.
2. Prophecy—v. 27. Jesus starts with Moses, and explains through the Prophets all the promises of His resurrection.
3. Person—vv. 28-29. Jesus stops to eat with the two disciples and reveals to them His identity.

Because Christ lives, we too shall live. Life is promised to all of His followers (John 11:25-26; note the words of John 3:16—"everlasting life"). He lives, and when He lives in our hearts, we too shall have abundant life (John 10:10), and eternal life (John 5:24).

39

AFTER EASTER

Luke 24:30-53

Many people are religious during Lent and at Easter. But, what happens after Easter? Notice what happend to the disciples after Easter. There was a change. They were better Christians. They were different people. Later, these same people changed their world.

I. THE FIRE—vv. 30-32

1. Fellowship—v. 30. Christ shares bread with the disciples.
2. Faith—v. 31. By faith they knew Christ arose, now their spiritual eyes are open and they know it is Christ.
3. Fire—v. 32. They rejoice as He explains the Scriptures.

II. THE FAITH—vv. 33-35
1. Proof—vv. 33-34. They tell how Christ has risen from the dead. They have proof. They know for sure.
2. People—v. 35. Two men from Emmaus tell how their hearts burned as Christ talked to them (see Mark 16:12).

III. THE FEAR—36-40
1. The Savior—v. 36. Christ appears and says, "Peace be unto you" (compare John 14:27).
2. The Scare—v. 37. They are fearful, thinking they are seeing a ghost. It was Jesus who had risen from the dead.
3. The Scars—vv. 38-40. Christ proves He is the Son of God. He shows the scars in His hands and feet.

IV. THE FELLOWSHIP—vv. 41-46
1. Reality—vv. 41-43. Here is proof that both His body and spirit arose from the dead. Can a spirit eat?
2. Reminder—vv. 44-46. Christ reminds them of the Scriptures. He speaks of the prophets' words being fulfilled. He opens their understanding (Acts 1:30; John 20:22). He tells of His resurrection.
3. Repentance—vv. 47-48. Repentance and remission of sins are to be preached, beginning at Jerusalem (compare with Acts 1:8).

V. THE FILLING—v. 49
1. Promise—"And behold, I send the promise of my Father unto you." The disciples would need power to carry on the work of the Lord.
2. Power—"But tarry ye in the city of Jerusalem, until ye be endued with power from on high." Later, we see the disciples and others receiving this power (Acts 2:1-4).

VI. THE FAITHFULNESS—vv. 50-53
1. Parting—vv. 50-51. After blessing the disciples, Christ ascends into heaven. Notice the words of the Savior before He goes into heaven (John 14:1-6). Luke also tells how He ascends (Acts 1:11).
2. Praising—vv. 52-53. They praise and worship the Lord. They were continually in the temple, worshiping and praising the Lord (see also Ps. 122:1; Heb. 10:25).

What does Christ mean to you? Do you know Him personally? Can you say, "He walks and talks with me." Have you made Him your Lord? Is He your Master? Does He have first place in your life? When Christ has first place in our lives, then *every day will be a holy day!*

DOLLAR SERMON LIBRARY

By Billy Apostolon
Choice Sermon Outlines
52 Invitation Illustrations
Heart-Stirring Sermon Outlines
Heart-Touching Sermon Outlines
Homiletic Outlines
Outlines for Evangelistic Sermons
Preach the Word
Soul-Winning Sermons
Special Days and Occasions

By Hyman Appelman
Evangelistic Sermons
Revival Sermons
Seeds for Sermons
Sermon Ideas and Outlines
Sermons on the Holy Spirit

By Adolph Bedsoie
Sermon Outlines on the Family and Home

By James Bolick
Sermon Outlines for Christian Living
Sermon Outlines for Revival Preaching
Sermon Outlines from the Word
Sermon Outlines on Paul and His Message

By George Brooks
Gospel Sermon Outlines

By Jeff D. Brown
Sermon Outlines on the Way of Salvation
Practical Sermon Outlines
Sermon Outlines on the Old Testament
Sermon Outlines on the Gospels and Acts
Sermon Outlines on the Letters to the Churches
Sermon Outlines on Timothy to Revelation

By J. D. Cameron
Sermon Outlines for Special Occasions

By W. H. Compton
50 Select Sermon Outlines
Funeral Sermon Outlines
Salvation Sermon Outlines
Vital Sermon Outlines

By Lash Frey and William Willis
Real Revival: Outlines for Sermons

By E. F. Hallock
Bible-Centered Sermon Starters
More Sermon Starters

By Eric Hayden
Complete Sermon Outlines

By Benjamin Horrell
Topical Sermon Outlines on Christ
Topical Sermon Outlines on I Corinthians
Topical Sermon Outlines on Romans

By James Inglis
Dynamic Sermon Starters
Suggested Sermon Starters

By Carl G. Johnson
Scriptural Sermon Outlines

By Wilbur B. Ketcham
Preacher's Toolbox

By Ian MacPherson
Live Sermon Outlines
Usable Outlines and Illustrations

By F. E. Marsh
Challenging Sermon Outlines and Bible Readings
More Sermon Outlines

By Croft M. Pentz
Christian Life Outlines
Expository Outlines on the Gospel of John
Expository Outlines from Luke
48 Simple Sermon Outlines
Outlines from Mark and Acts
Sermon Outlines for Christians
Prayer Meeting Outlines
Sermon Outlines From the Psalms
Sermon Outlines on the Epistles, Romans — II Corinthians
Sermon Outlines on the Epistles, Titus — Jude
Sunday Morning Sermon Outlines

By A. T. Pierson
Outline Studies of Great Texts and Themes from the Bible

By Joel T. Slayton
New Testament Sermon Outlines

By Charles H. Spurgeon, and Others
Ready Sermon Outlines

By Paul Tassell
Outline Studies in Jeremiah

By Richard S. Taylor
Timely Sermon Outlines

By R. A. Torrey
Suggestive Sermon Outlines

By Nathaniel A. Urshan
Harvestime Sermons

By C. M. Ward
Revivaltime Sermons

BAKER BOOK HOUSE, Grand Rapids, Michigan